Bass for the Absolute Beginner

Absolutely everything you need to know to start playing now!

Joe Bouchard

Alfred, the leader in educational publishing,
and the National Guitar Workshop,
one of America's finest guitar schools, have joined
forces to bring you the best, most progressive
educational tools possible. We hope you will enjoy
this book and encourage you to look for
other fine products from Alfred and the
National Guitar Workshop.

ISBN 0-7390-2369-1 (Book)
ISBN 0-7390-2370-5 (Book and CD)
ISBN 0-7390-2371-3 (CD)

*This book was acquired, edited and produced
by Workshop Arts, Inc., the publishing arm of
the National Guitar Workshop.
Nathaniel Gunod, acquisitions and editor
Michael Rodman, editor
Gary Tomassetti, music typesetter
Timothy Phelps, interior design
CD recorded at Bar None Studios, Northford, CT*

*Large Bass photograph: Fender P-Bass, courtesy of
Fender Musical Instruments Corporation*

Table of Contents

If you have the optional CD for this book, you can tune your bass to the tuning notes on the first track. Every example that is recorded on the CD is marked with this symbol.

Track 1

About the Author

Joe Bouchard is one of the founding members of legendary rock band, Blue Öyster Cult. He was a creative member of the group for 16 years, recording 13 albums for Columbia Records and being awarded nine gold and two platinum albums. Some of his famous bass lines, such as those on *Don't Fear the Reaper, Godzilla* and *Burnin for You,* are still heard daily on classic rock radio.

After leaving Blue Öyster Cult in 1986, Joe performed as organist and pianist with Spencer Davis of the Spencer Davis Group. In 1998, the popular heavy metal group Metallica recorded Joe's song, *Astronomy,* on their multiplatinum CD "Garage Inc."

In 2001 he produced a CD entitled "Bouchard, Dunaway and Smith, Back From Hell" which features former Alice Cooper members Dennis Dunaway and Neal Smith, with several songs co-written with Ian Hunter.

Joe spends much of his time teaching students guitar, bass guitar and piano. He is the author of several educational music books, including *Rock Guitar for Beginners*, *Beginning Rock Keyboard* and *Intermediate Rock Keyboard*, published by National Guitar Workshop and Alfred Publishing. Alfred also distributes his instructional video, *Rock Bass for Beginners*.

Joe holds a Bachelor of Music Education from Ithaca College and a Master of Music from The Hartt School at the University of Hartford. Joe has taught at the National Guitar Workshop and now teaches privately, and produces commercial music for radio and television.

Acknowledgments

Thanks to Nat Gunod, Dave Smolover and everyone at the National Guitar Workshop. Also, thanks to Ron Manus, Link Harnsberger and the gang at Alfred Publishing.

Introduction

Congratulations! You have taken the first step in learning how to play the electric bass. The bass is more popular than ever, with students of all ages picking it up. It's a simple fact that in order to have a great band, you need a solid bass player. So you're already in demand!

This book will teach you everything you need to know to get playing right away and make your band sound great.

Getting Started

● Shopping for Your Electric Bass

All modern music stores sell bass guitars. They come in all different shapes, sizes and colors. When trying out a bass, ask a salesperson for assistance. The bass need not be expensive. An electric bass can cost up to $2000 or more, but a good beginner's model, which will last a long time, can be found in the $175 to $375 price range.

Two popular electric basses

Small Practice Amp

In order to hear the low tones of a bass, you will need a small practice amp. These are great for practicing around the house and some include a headphone jack for ultra-quiet practicing. You will also need a guitar cable to connect your bass to the amplifier.

Practice amp and cable with bass

● Holding the Bass

Posture is very important. Good posture will result in better endurance (being able to play longer), better focus and probably better playing overall. Keep the following in mind:

• Your back should be straight and upright.
• Breathe and focus.
• The bass should be high enough on your torso to allow free access to all of the strings and frets.

These points may seem obvious, but they are very important. If you slouch or forget to breathe deeply, you will not be able to play as well.

Seated

Standing

● Parts of the Bass

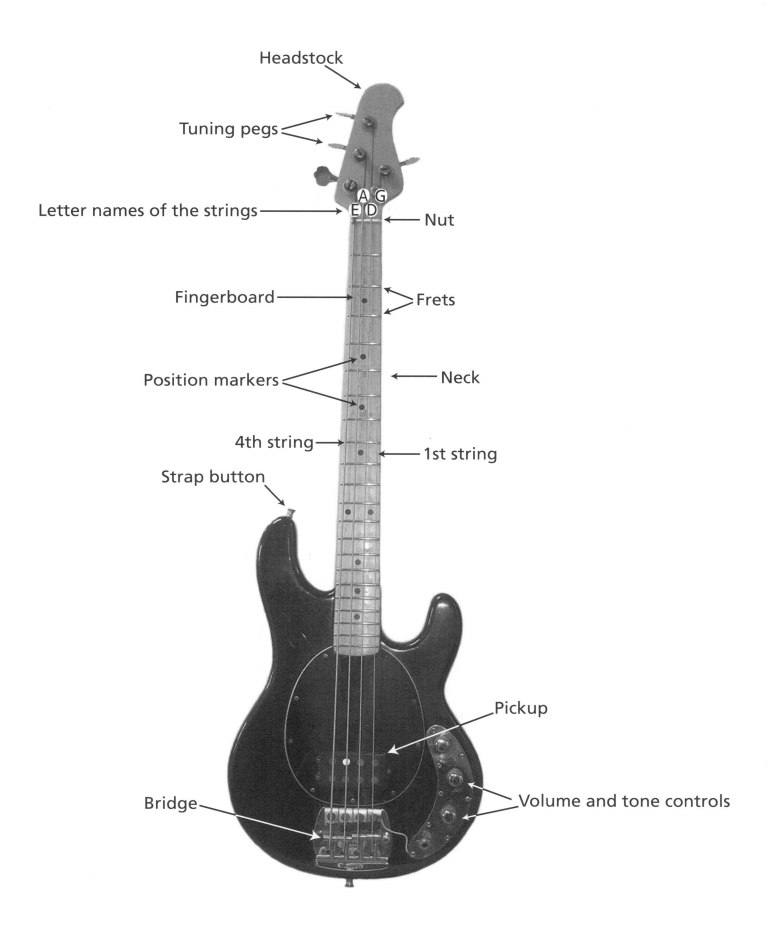

Headstock

Tuning pegs

Letter names of the strings

Nut

Fingerboard

Frets

Position markers

Neck

4th string

1st string

Strap button

Pickup

Bridge

Volume and tone controls

● Tuning the Bass

The first time you play the bass, it is probably best to get someone to tune it for you. If you buy the bass in a store, have the salesperson tune it.

Your bass will need to be tuned almost every time you play it. It may have been in tune when you first bought it, but moving it around, and other factors, will cause it to go out of tune. Several ways to tune a bass are disussed below.

Remember that you can tune your bass to the tuning notes in Track 1 of the CD that is available for this book.

Track 1

Digital Tuners

Inexpensive electronic digital tuners are very popular and very helpful since the low-pitched tones of the bass are sometimes difficult to hear. To tune using this method, you merely plug your cable into the input jack on the tuner and read the display on the front. The display will tell you if you need to tighten or loosen the string using the tuning peg. The tighter the string, the higher it sounds; the looser it is, the lower it sounds. Check the manual that comes with the tuner if you are uncertain how the tuner operates.

Relative Tuning

If you don't have an electronic tuner, you can still tune your bass using *relative tuning*. Using this method, we tune the strings relative to one another.

- Tune the 4th string (E) to a low tone that allows the string to be heard without putting too much tension on it. Even better, tune it to a low E from another instrument, such as the 6th string of your friend's guitar. The 6th string on a guitar is also an E, although it is higher sounding than your 4th string should sound. You'll have to do this if you want to play in tune with your friend.

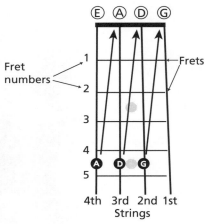

- Tune the 3rd string (A) to the sound of the 4th string played at the 5th fret.

- Tune the 2nd string (D) to the sound of the 3rd string played at the 5th fret.

- Tune the 1st string (G) to the sound of the 2nd string played at the 5th fret.

This method is a good way to check your tuning quickly.

Tuning to a Keyboard

You can tune all four strings using a keyboard, or just use the keyboard to tune your 4th string and use relative tuning for the rest. Simply match the sound of your strings to the correct notes on the keyboard (shown in the diagram below).

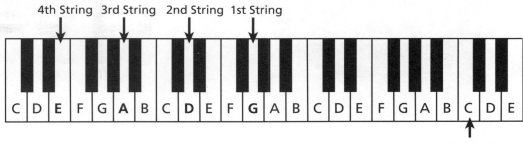

● Right-Hand Technique

There are two basic styles of playing a bass guitar: pickstyle and fingerstyle. Both are commonly used and the style used usually depends on the type of music being played. Pickstyle is dominant in rock music, fingerstyle is used more for jazz or funk music. This is hardly a rule, however, since players often choose one playing style over the other as a matter of personal preference, regardless of musical style.

Pickstyle

To play pickstyle, hold the pick firmly between your thumb and index finger (see photo on the right). Then, use the pick to pluck the strings with either a downstroke ⊓ (toward the floor) or an upstroke ∨ (toward the ceiling).

Pickstyle playing gives the bass player a hard-edge sound that is great for rock music. It also is good when you need to play a very fast passage powerfully.

Holding the pick

> ⊓ = Downstroke with the pick
> ∨ = Upstroke with the pick

Plucking a string with the pick

Fingerstyle

Fingerstyle bass is very popular. Using your fingers gives you a wide range of tones. From jazz to funk, fingers rule.

To play fingerstyle, anchor your thumb on the edge of the pickguard or the edge of a pickup and pull the strings toward you, alternating the index finger (*i*) with the middle finger (*m*). For the 3rd string (A), 2nd string (D) and 1st string (G), we use a technique called *rest stroke*. After playing a string, the finger lands on the next adjacent string. With the 4th string (E), the finger might strike the body of the bass. This is natural and allows the finger to get a more solid tone from the string.

Before a rest stroke

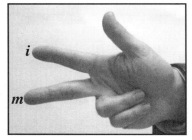

The index (i) and middle (m) fingers

After a rest stroke

● Left-Hand Technique

Left-hand finger numbers:
1 = index
2 = middle
3 = ring finger
4 = pinkie or little finger

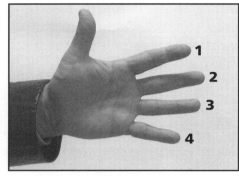

The left-hand fingers

Left-hand fingers should be placed on the strings just behind (to the left of) the frets. Do not place the fingers directly on top of the frets, because this creates a muted, unclear tone. Placing them just behind the fret will create a clear tone.

Place the left-hand fingers directly behind the frets.

●The Musical Alphabet

Music notes are given letter names: A, B, C, D, E, F and G.   This is called the *musical alphabet*. After the letter G, the sequence starts again with A to G, and so on, until you reach the highest note on your instrument.

> **The Musical Alphabet**
> A B C D E F G A B C D E F G A B C...and so on.

To start learning music notes on your bass, you first need to learn the names of the strings. They are, from lowest-sounding to highest-sounding: E, A, D and G. The E is the 4th string and closest to the ceiling. The A is the 3rd string, D is the 2nd string and G is the 1st string and closest to the floor.

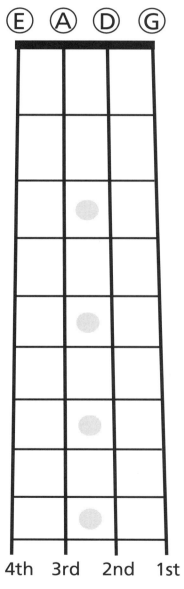

4th   3rd   2nd   1st

Get Started Playing

● Warming Up—Finger Style

Before we dig into playing some serious bass, it is a good idea to warm up your fingers. This will help you get a feel for the strings, and should be done first everytime you play.

Play the following open strings with your right hand, alternating the *i* and *m* fingers. Count aloud at a relaxed pace as you pluck each string. Play eight notes on the 3rd string and then on to the 2nd string. After playing the 1st string move your arm so that the fingers are positioned on the 4th string. Play the 4th string, and finally, return to the 3rd string.

Play this warm-up exercise ten times. Then rest a few minutes and play again. Try to make the tones the two right-hand fingers produce sound identical.

Track 2

Fingerstyle Warm-Up

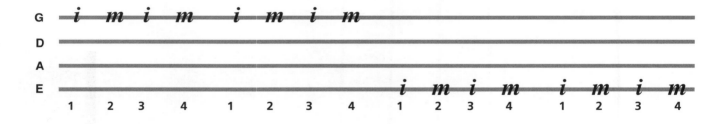

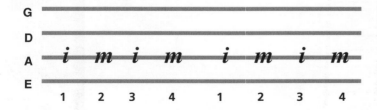

● Tablature (TAB)

Tablature, or TAB for short, is a popular method of writing music for the bass. Numbers (representing frets) are placed on lines (representing strings) to show which fret to play on which string. The bottom line of the TAB represents the 4th string; the third line from the top represents the 3rd string; the second line represents the 2nd string; the top line of represents the 1st string.

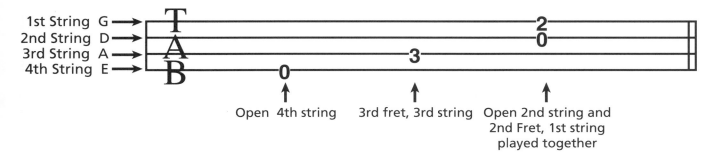

1st String G →
2nd String D →
3rd String A →
4th String E →

Open 4th string   3rd fret, 3rd string   Open 2nd string and
2nd Fret, 1st string
played together

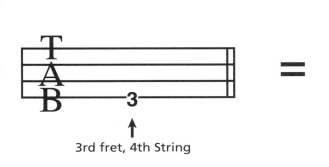

3rd fret, 4th String

Paul McCartney played bass with The Beatles in the 1960s, his solo group, Wings, in the 1970s and other solo projects in the 1980s and 1990s. His fluid bass style and flawless musicianship continues to influence contemporary bass players.

● Rhythm (Musical Time)

Note Values and Beats

As the bass player in the band, it will be your job to work with the drummer to make people want to tap their toes or get up and dance. But first, you must understand the basics of musical time, which we call *rhythm*.

Some notes last longer than others. It is the combination of longer and shorter notes that creates rhythm. In written music, this is shown with different *note values*. Let's start with three: the *whole note*, *half note* and *quarter note*.

To understand note values you must understand *beats*. Beats are equal divisions of musical time. They are the basic unit of measure—and the pulse that keeps the music alive. As the chart on the right illustrates, each note value has a specific length that is measured in beats.

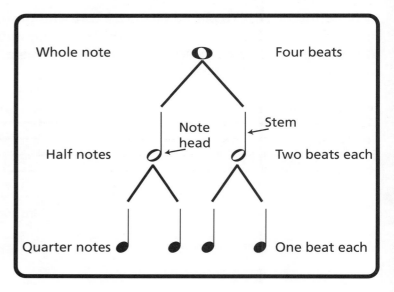

Measures and Time Signatures

These rhythm values are organized in rhythmic units called *measures*, which are marked by *bar lines*. A *time signature*, shown at the beginning of a piece of music, is used to indicate how many beats should be in each measure. The most common time signature is $\frac{4}{4}$. The four on top means that every measure will have four beats; the four on the bottom stands for a quarter note, which is what tells us the quarter note is the note value receiving one beat.

$\frac{4}{4}$ = Four beats per measure
$\frac{4}{4}$ = A quarter note ♩ gets one beat

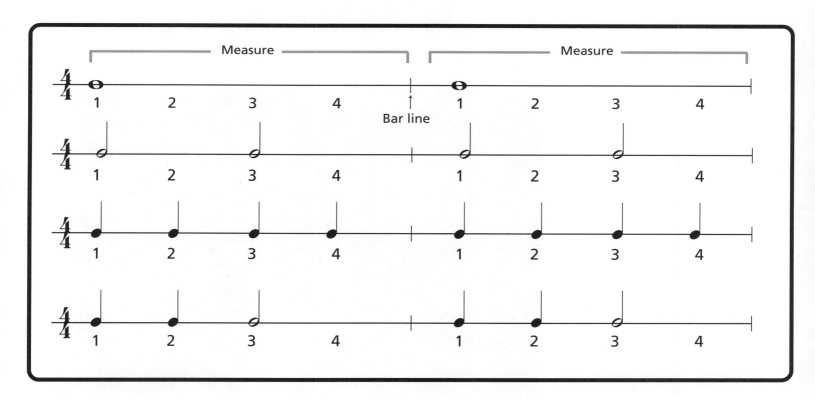

Playing in Time

Let's get ready to play your first song, which is on the following page. Below are three lines of music written in TAB.

Play Example 1 slowly. It involves just the 3rd string. Try both styles of playing: fingerstyle, alternating *i* and *m*; and pickstyle, alternating downstrokes ⊓ and upstrokes ⋁.

When you've mastered Example 1, go on to Examples 2 and 3. Example 2 is played on the 2nd string. Example 3 alternates two beats on the 3rd string and two beats on the 2nd string.

Notice the sign at the far right side of each example. A thick line, a thin line and two dots combine to create a *repeat sign*. This sign simply tells you to play the music again. Also notice that the time signature and note values are written above the tablature.

Example 1

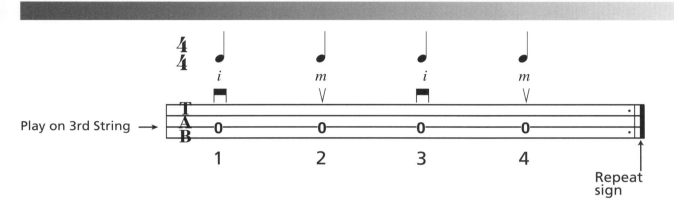

Example 2

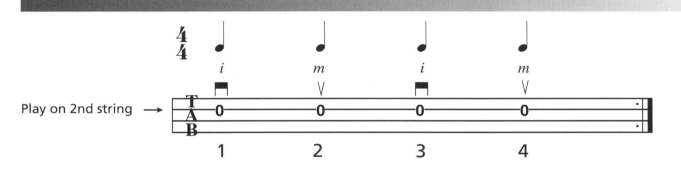

Example 3

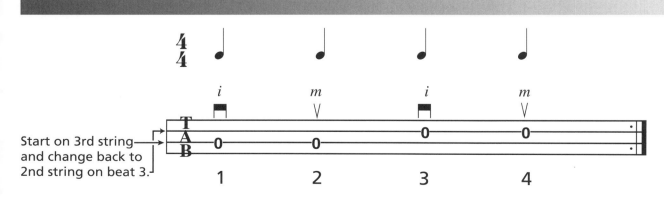

Here's your first song. Count as you play at a moderate pace. Also, notice the *final double bar* at the end. This kind of bar line is used to show when a tune is over. Enjoy!

Track 3

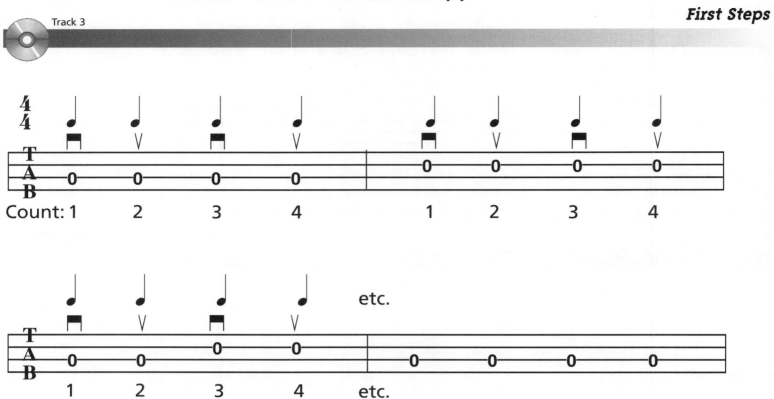

Count: 1   2   3   4   1   2   3   4

etc.

1   2   3   4   etc.

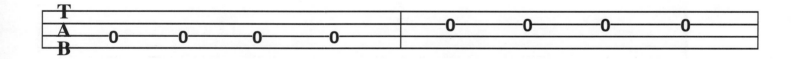

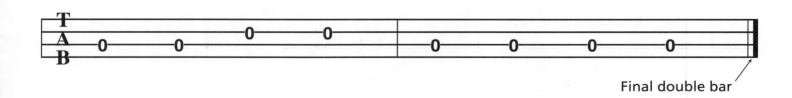

Final double bar

●Reading Standard Notation

To become a well-rounded player, you need to know how to read standard music notation. Note symbols such as those introduced on page 12 are placed on a *staff*, which consists of five lines and four spaces.

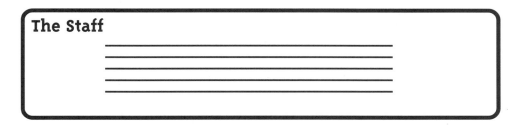

The Staff

At the beginning of each staff line of music, there is a symbol called a *clef*. The *bass clef* 𝄢 is also called the *F clef*, since the symbol has two dots that surround the "F" line.

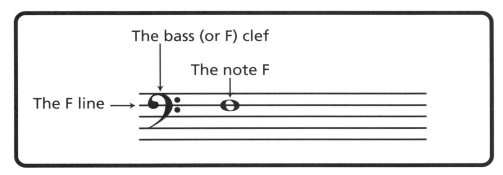

The bass (or F) clef

The note F

The F line →

Notes are placed on the lines *and* the spaces. The lines of the bass clef (from the bottom line up) are the notes G–B–D–F–A (often memorized as "**G**ood **B**oys **D**o **F**ine **A**lways"). The spaces (from the bottom space up) are the notes A–C–E–G ("**A**ll **C**ows **E**at **G**rass"). Notes that are higher or lower than the staff are written on *ledger lines* that extend the staff up or down. The lowest note used in this book is the low E, which is on the first ledger line below the staff. This is the note of the open 4th string on the bass.

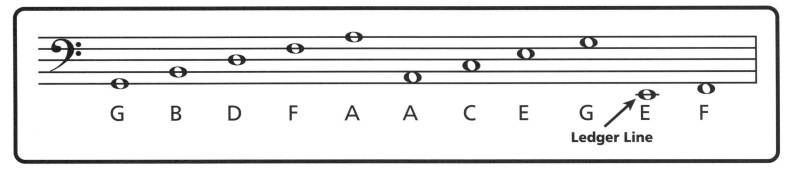

G   B   D   F   A   A   C   E   G   E   F

Ledger Line

Here are all the notes on the bass staff, from the lowest note on the bass to the highest note on the staff, in sequence from the bottom up. Note the double bar at the end. This is used to indicate the end of a section or short exercise.

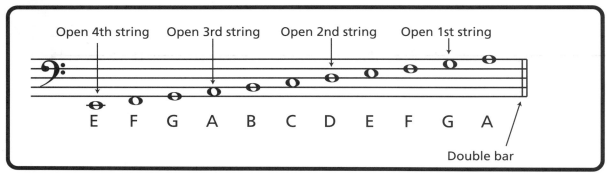

Open 4th string   Open 3rd string   Open 2nd string   Open 1st string

E   F   G   A   B   C   D   E   F   G   A

Double bar

Most TAB has standard notation written above it. Study the example below to see the correlation between TAB and the bass staff.

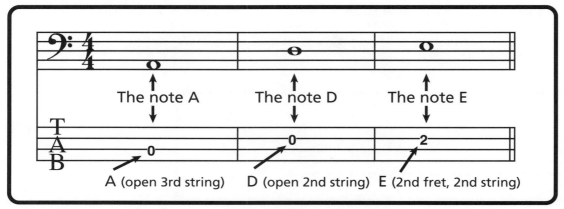

The note A   The note D   The note E

A (open 3rd string)   D (open 2nd string)   E (2nd fret, 2nd string)

This next easy song mixes quarter notes and half notes. Be sure to count two beats for each half note. For now, the names of the notes are shown above the music. You can choose to play pickstyle or fingerstyle. Indications for both are given. Keep the pace moderate.

Track 4

Next Steps

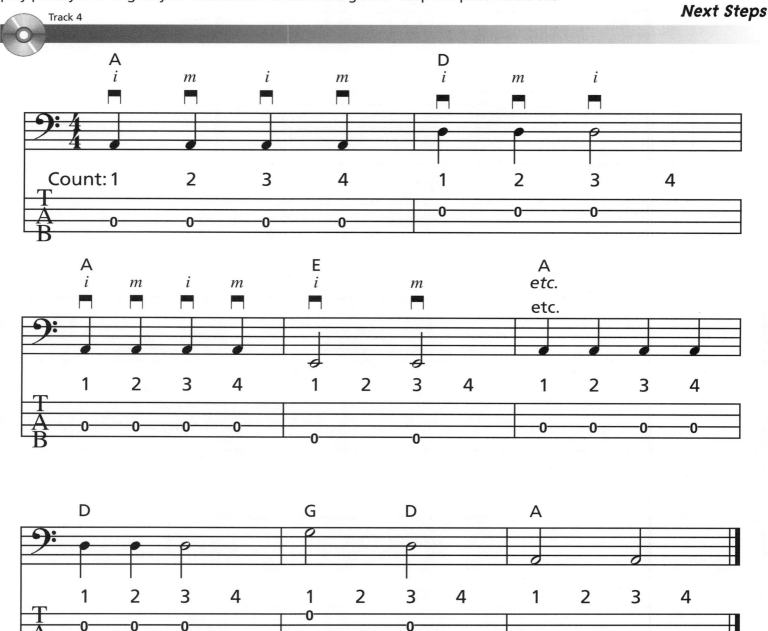

Here is a song that uses quarter notes, half notes and whole notes. Remember, a whole note sustains for four beats. To to think of the name for each note as you play.

Classic Track

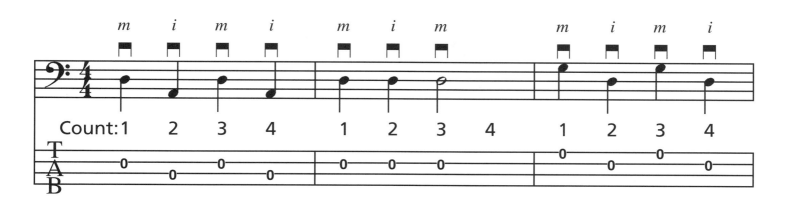

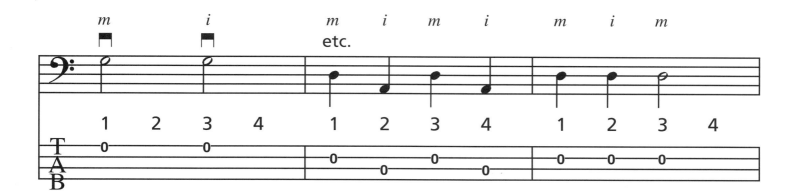

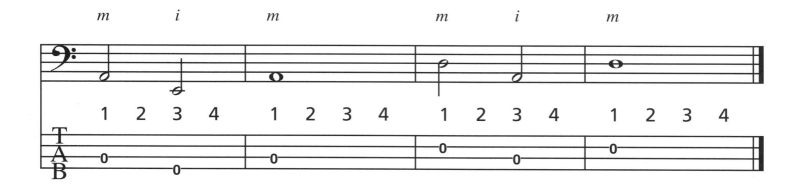

● Rests

If notes were played continuously with no breaks or silences, music would become monotonous. *Rests* add a silence to the music. It is like giving the listener (not to mention the singer) time to take a breath.

Here are some rests:

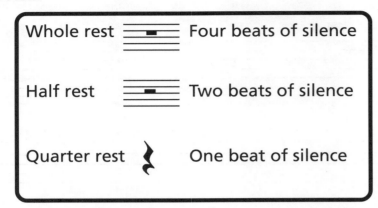

Whole rest		Four beats of silence
Half rest		Two beats of silence
Quarter rest		One beat of silence

Below is an example of a musical passage with rests and the corresponding TAB. One reason that TAB is not as accurate as standard music notation is that it does not include rests. Where the rests occur is usually left blank in TAB.

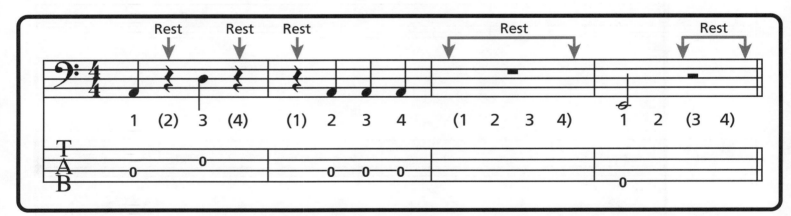

Important Note

When playing a note followed by a rest, deaden the string by putting your left hand lightly on the string to stop the vibration (which will stop the note). The rhythm of the rest must be accurate—if the rest is on the second beat, the string must be deadened exactly on the second beat.

Below is a song that uses the notes and quarter rests. If you play this pickstyle, use downstrokes. To play it fingerstyle, use *i* and *m* as indicated. Be sure to count the notes and rests, and don't play too fast.

Easy Going

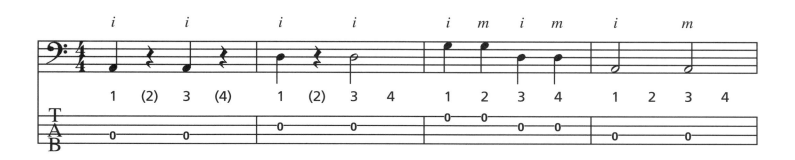

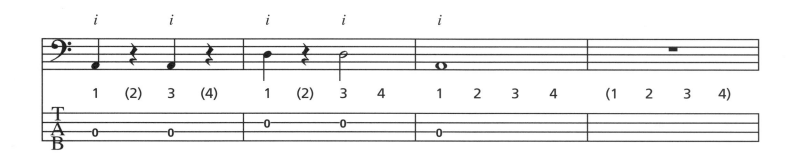

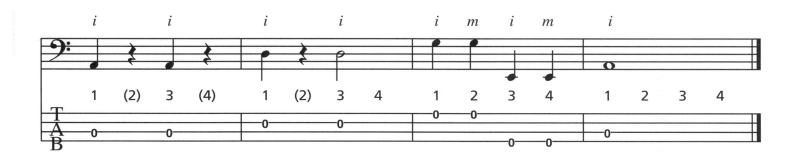

Review Worksheet No. 1

A. Draw the notes and rests below and tell how many beats.

      1. Draw a whole note _____ = _____ beat(s)

      2. Draw a half note_____ = _____ beat(s)

      3. Draw a quarter note _____ = _____ beat(s)

      4. Draw a quarter rest _____ = _____ beat(s)

      5. Draw a half rest _____ = _____ beat(s)

      6. Draw a whole rest _____ = _____ beat(s)

B.

On the TAB below write the fret and the note name of the string it is on:

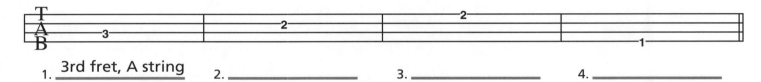

    1. 3rd fret, A string   2. _____   3. _____   4. _____

C. Fill in the blanks

      1. How many beats are in a measure of $\frac{4}{4}$? _____

      2. In $\frac{4}{4}$, what kind of note gets one beat? _____

      3. What kind of rest gets one beat? _____

      4. What kind of rest gets four beats? _____

      5. When using relative tuning, what fret is used to compare a string with the next string? _____

D. Spell words below the staff by writing the note names.

    1. _____   2. _____   3. _____   4. _____

    5. _____   6. _____   7. _____   8. _____

New Notes and Rhythms

● Eighth Notes ♪

The next important note value to learn is the *eighth note*. Just as half notes are half as long as whole notes, and quarter notes are half as long as half notes, eighth notes are half as long as quarter notes. Eighth notes are the backbone of most rock bass parts.

It is helpful to notice that when you tap your foot to the beat, there are two parts to the movement: the "up" motion and the "down" motion. Those are the two halves of a beat.

To count eighth notes, count "1 & (and), 2 &, 3 &, 4 &," and so on.

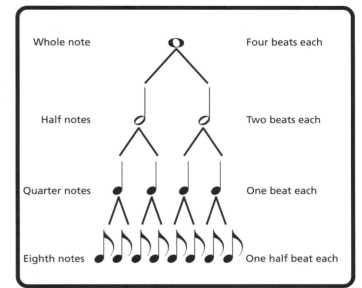

Single eighth notes have a *flag*. When consecutive eighth notes are written, a *beam* connects them. Count and play (pickstyle and fingerstyle) the following examples of eighth-note patterns.

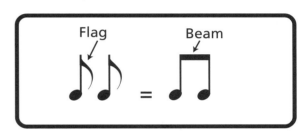

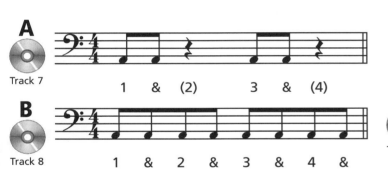

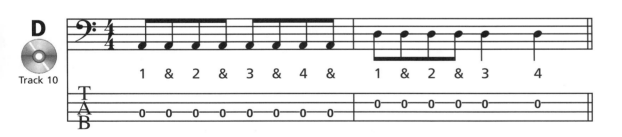

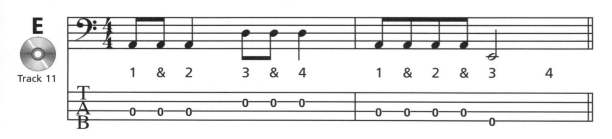

● B and C on the 3rd String

This is a good time to go back to page 7 and review left-hand technique.

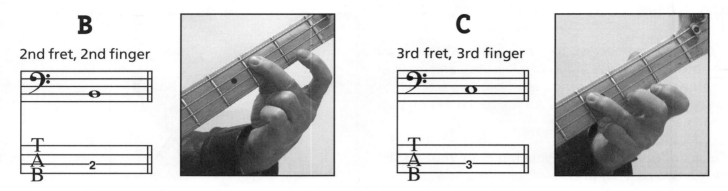

B

2nd fret, 2nd finger

C

3rd fret, 3rd finger

Let's try out these new notes with the following exercise.

Example 4

Track 12

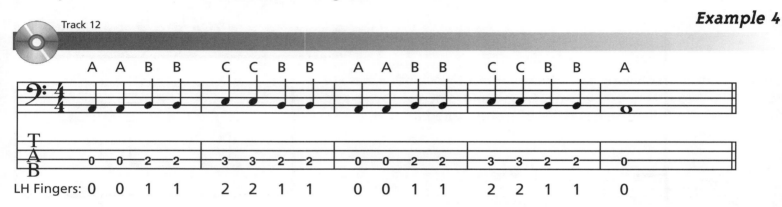

A A B B C C B B A A B B C C B B A

LH Fingers: 0 0 1 1   2 2 1 1   0 0 1 1   2 2 1 1   0

Below is a tune that uses eighth notes. You can play either fingerstyle or pickstyle, or try it both ways. Dig in!

Eighth-Note Tune

Track 13

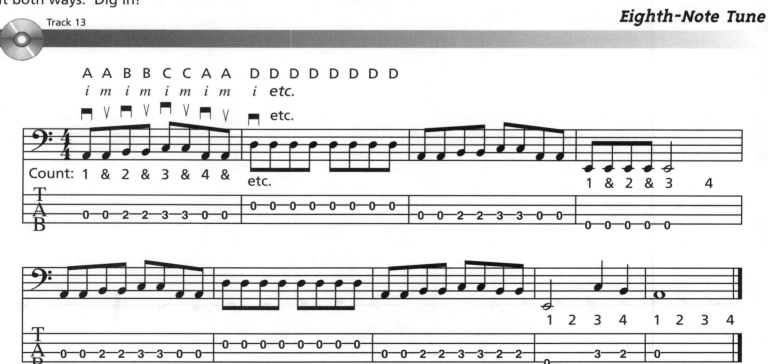

Introducing E and F on the 2nd String

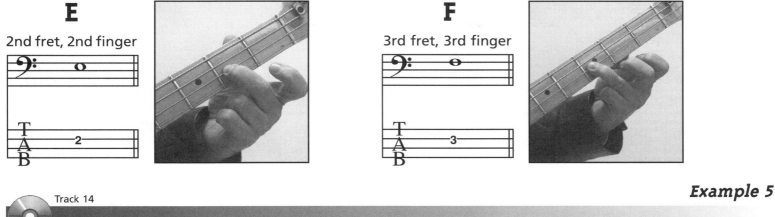

E
2nd fret, 2nd finger

F
3rd fret, 3rd finger

Track 14

Example 5

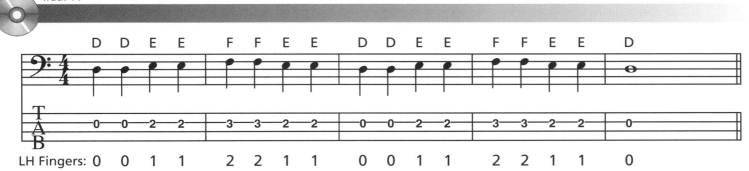

The Eighth Rest ⅞

An eighth rest ⅞ lasts for one half beat.

Example 6 uses eighth rests and E and F on the 2nd string. Notice that in this song, there is more to play after the repeat sign. The second time through, continue past the repeat sign to the final double bar. This is very common.

Track 15

Example 6

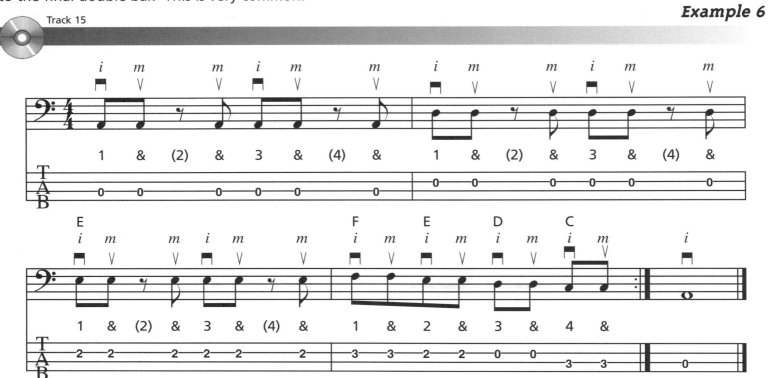

Here is a quicker tune with eighth notes. At the end of the second line, two eighth rests are
used rather than a quarter note rest to make it easier to see the fourth beat in the measure.

Track 16

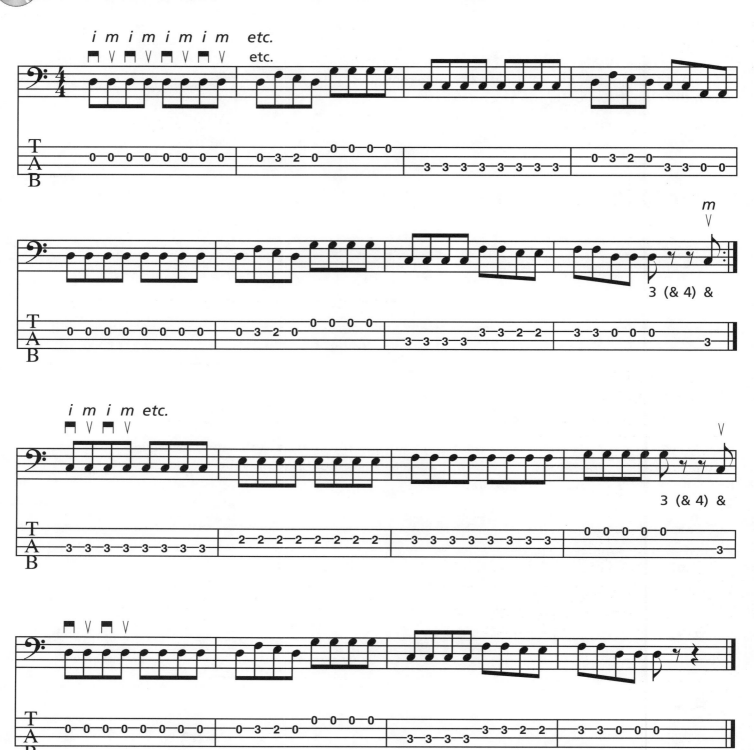

Ties, Dots and More New Notes

● Ties

A *tie* allows us to extend the duration of a note by adding its value to another note's value. A tie is a simple curved line, ⌒ or ⌣, drawn from one note head to the next. The second note in a tie is not struck. Rather, the first note continues to sustain through the value of the second note.

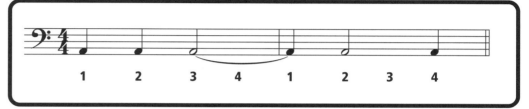

This makes it possible for us to play a note that is longer than one measure, or to play a note that is three beats long when there are only two beats left in a measure.

● Dotted Half Notes 𝅗𝅥.

Another way of extending a note's time value is to add a *dot*. A dot to the right of a note indicates that the note's value is increased by one half. For example, a half note gets two beats, and half of that value is one beat. So, a *dotted half note* gets three beats. You can also think of it this way: A dotted half note is equal to a half note tied to a quarter note.

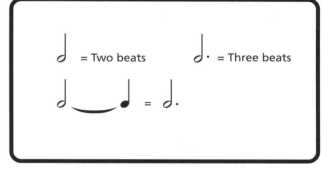

Flea is the bassist with the Red Hot Chili Peppers. He has also played on other artists' records, such as Young MC's Bust A Move (1989) and Alanis Morrisette's You Oughta Know (1995).

This song uses dotted half notes. Count aloud to get the correct rhythm. There is also a tie in the last two measures. Hold the last note for six beats. This tune should move pretty quickly.

 Track 17

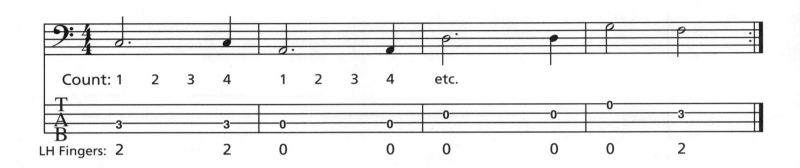

Count: 1   2   3   4   1   2   3   4   etc.

LH Fingers: 2   2   0   0   0   0   0   2

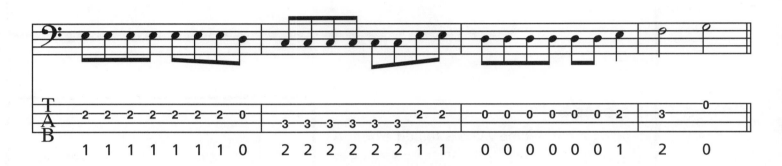

1 1 1 1 1 1 1 0   2 2 2 2 2 2 1 1   0 0 0 0 0 0 1   2   0

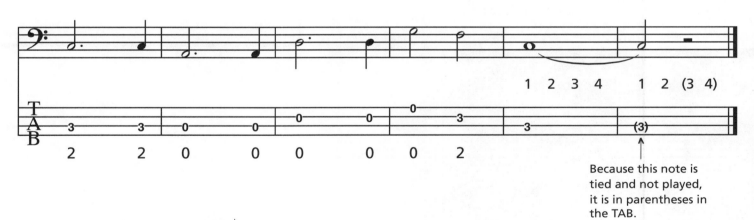

2   2   0   0   0   0   0   2

1 2 3 4   1 2 (3 4)

Because this note is tied and not played, it is in parentheses in the TAB.

● Dotted Quarter Notes ♩.

Dotted quarter notes work just like dotted half notes: The dot increases the note's value by one half. Half of a quarter note is half a beat, so a dotted quarter note gets one and a half beats. For that reason, a dotted quarter note note is often followed by an eighth note. The dotted quarter is equal to three eighth notes.

Count: 1 & 2 & 3   4

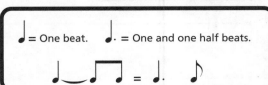

♩ = One beat.   ♩. = One and one half beats.

● F and G on the 4th String

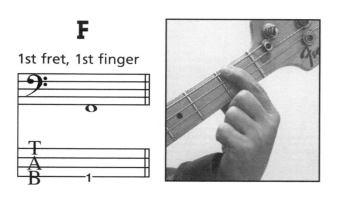

F

1st fret, 1st finger

G

3rd fret, 3rd finger

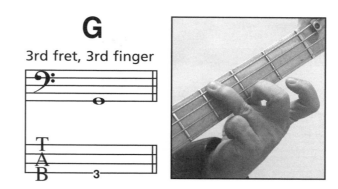

Track 18

Example 7

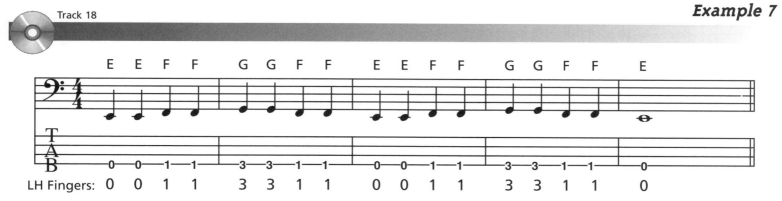

LH Fingers: 0 0 1 1   3 3 1 1   0 0 1 1   3 3 1 1 0

More about Repeats

You have already learned this sign ‖, which is a left-facing repeat. A left-facing repeat has dots on the left and tells you to go back to the beginning and play again. But it can also mean to go back to the most recent right-facing repeat sign, which has the dots on the right, ‖. When you see a right-facing repeat, keep playing past it, taking note of where it is, and then come back to it when you reach the left-facing repeat sign.

This song has a bouncy pop feel. Don't forget to repeat each line of music. Feel the groove!

Downtown Rebound

Track 19

Here is another song that uses dotted quarter notes. This tune is a great example of how the dotted quarter note/eighth note combination is one of the basic rock rhythms. Pick down on the dotted quarters and up on the eighths, or just alternate *i* and *m*. This tune moves pretty quickly.

Track 20

Primal Rock

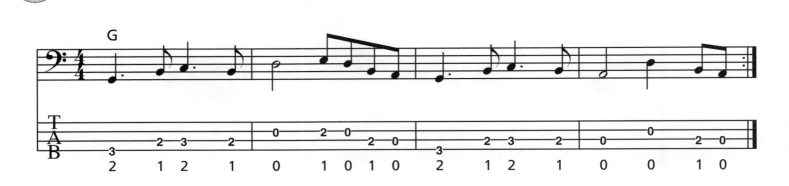

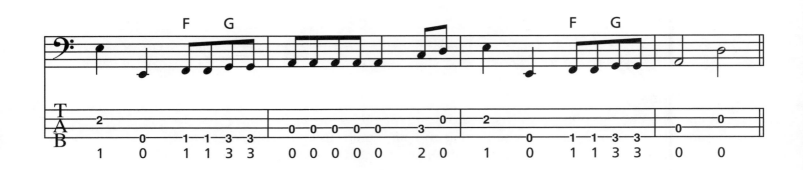

Here is a lively song that uses dotted rhythms.

Steady Groove

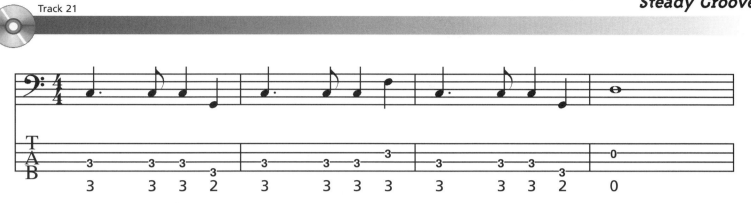

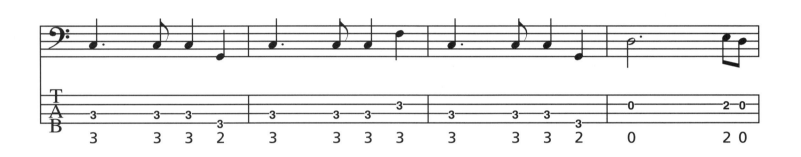

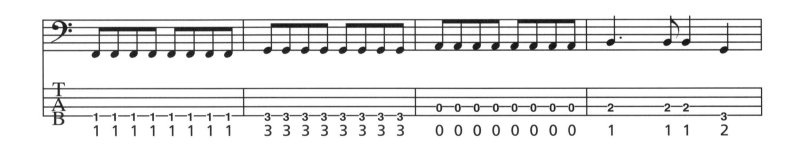

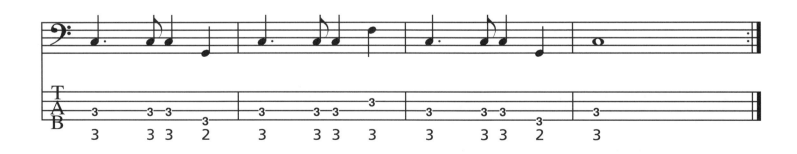

Your First Accidental—The Sharp ♯

An *accidental* is a sign used to raise, lower or return a note to its original *pitch* (pitch is the highness or lowness of sound). A sharp sign ♯ placed on the same line or space before a note indicates the pitch has been raised one fret. For example, there is an F at the 3rd fret, 2nd string. F♯ ("F sharp") is at the 4th fret, 2nd string. An accidental remains in force throughout the measure in which it appears.

F♯ and C♯

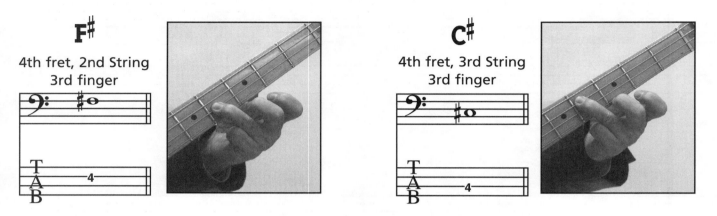

F♯

4th fret, 2nd String
3rd finger

C♯

4th fret, 3rd String
3rd finger

Most of the examples and songs we've played so far are *accompaniment* parts—they are typical of bass parts that accompany a melody. But we can play melodies on the bass. Melodies on the bass have a way of "jumping out" at the listener. In jazz songs, the bass may even play an entire *chorus* (in jazz terminology, this means "one time through" a song) or more, playing an improvised melody.

Let's play a couple of simple melodies. Here is *Twinkle, Twinkle, Little Star*, arranged for bass. This song uses the F♯ on the 2nd string and the C♯ on the 3rd string.

Track 22

Twinkle, Twinkle, Little Star

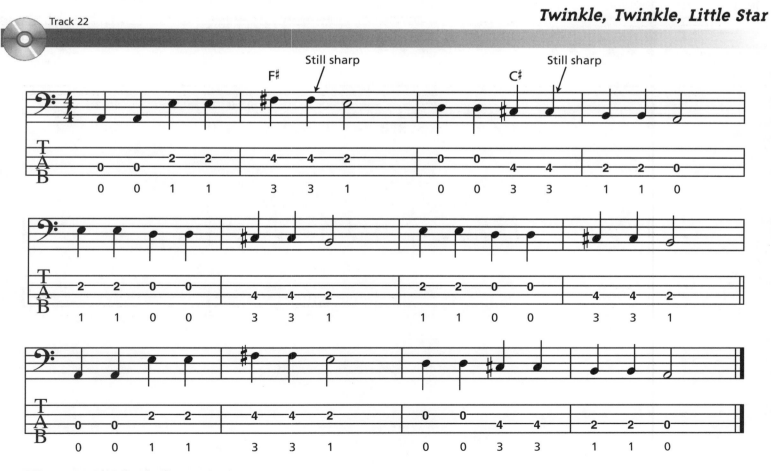

Introducing A and B on the 1st String

A

2nd fret, 1st finger

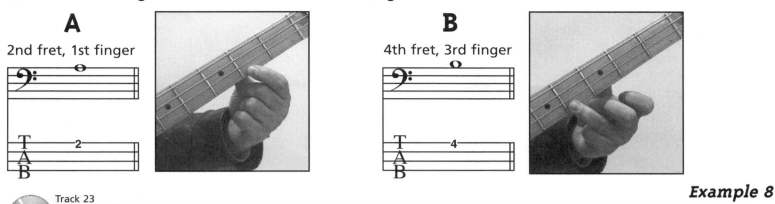

B

4th fret, 3rd finger

Track 23

Example 8

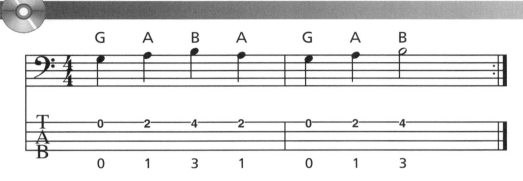

Pickups and Incomplete Measures

A *pickup* is a note (or notes) that occur before the first complete measure of a piece. In *Auld Lang Syne*, there is one beat before the first full measure. Because there is one extra beat at the beginning, the last measure of the song has only three beats. These are called *incomplete measures*.

Here is another popular song arranged for bass. Often heard on New Year's Eve, it is a seasonal favorite.

Auld Lang Syne

Track 24

Often, the bass will have a continuous groove up until a point where the band stops. Then, the bass jumps in with a melody.

In *Lead the Pack*, you have an accompaniment groove (the first line) followed by a four-measure solo starting at measure 5. The groove returns at the end. Don't forget to repeat measures 1–2, 3–4 and 9–10. The measures are numbered at the beginning of the second, third and fourth lines. This one moves at a moderate pace.

Track 25

This next song has a short solo (sometimes called a *break*) at the end of each four-measure *phrase* (a complete musical idea). When we speak, we acknowledge phrases, often taking short pauses between ideas. Musical phrases are also separated, sometimes by longer notes, other times by rests, or by a clear change of some other kind. In this tune, eighth-note rests and short breaks define the phrases. It's not a very fast tune, but play with energy!

Track 26

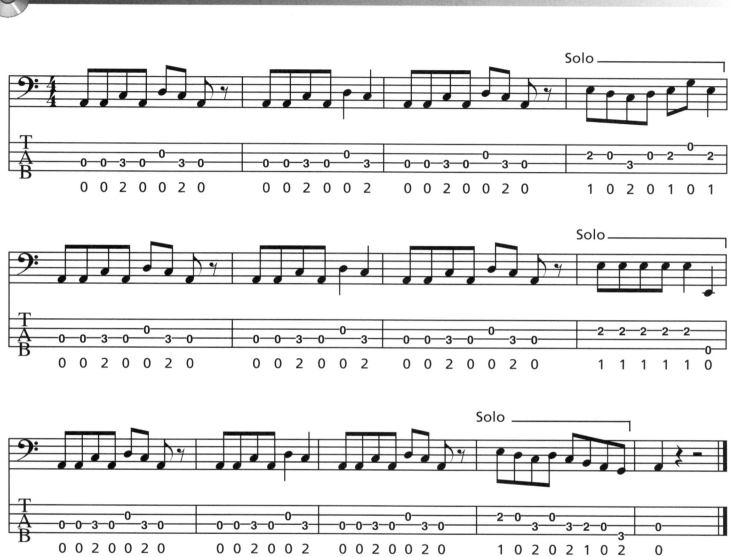

Theory

● Whole Steps and Half Steps

In music, the distance between two notes is called an *interval*. The simplest intervals are the *whole step* (a distance of two frets) and the *half step* (a distance of one fret).

Below are diagrams of whole steps and half steps on the bass fretboard and the keyboard. (Sometimes, seeing musical ideas expressed on a keyboard can help make them more clear.)

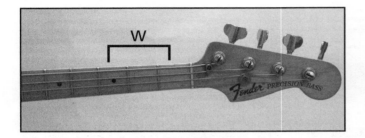
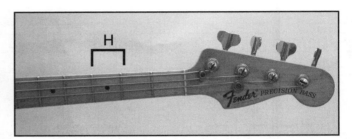

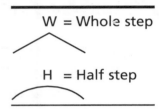

W = Whole step

H = Half step

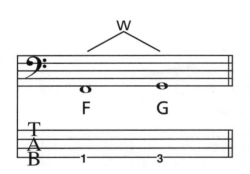
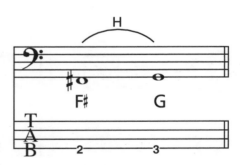

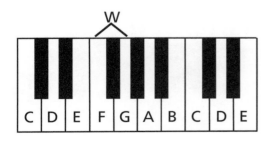
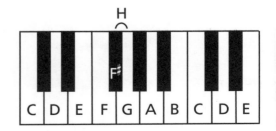

● The Major Scale and High Notes

In order to understand the basic building blocks of harmony, one needs to learn *scales*. A scale is an arrangement of notes in a specific order of whole steps and half steps that always move in order through the musical alphabet. Most scales contain seven different notes, and then finish with the same note on which they began. The most basic scale is the C Major scale.

To learn the C Major scale, you need to learn high C on the 1st string. This will require the use of your left-hand 4th finger (the pinkie). Using the 4th finger can be a little awkward at first, so take it slowly.

High C

5th fret, 1st string
4th finger

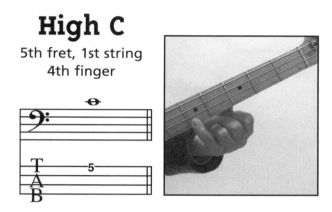

Below are the notes for a C Major Scale. Note the pattern of whole steps and half steps All major scales are structured this way, so this is known as the *formula* for the major scale.

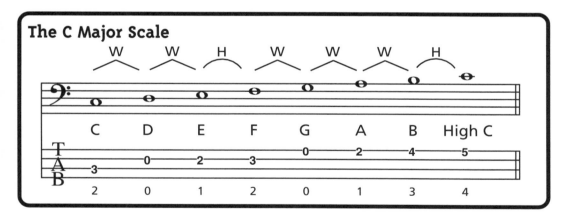

Practicing scales is great for building technique on the bass or any instrument. Play the scale above up and down (forward and backward) several times until you feel solid on each note.

The major scale is also the basis for many other elements of music theory, so make sure you know the formula well.

Here are two more major scales and some new notes to get you started on the road to major-scale knowledge. Notice that only the C Major scale has no accidentals. When we start a major scale on any other note, we must add accidentals to stay within the major scale formula.

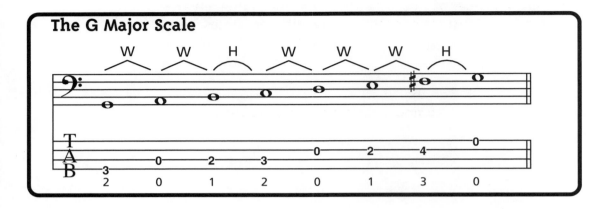

The D Major Scale introduces two more important notes: High C# and the high D.

High C#

6th fret, 1st String
4th finger

High D

7th fret, 1st String
4th finger

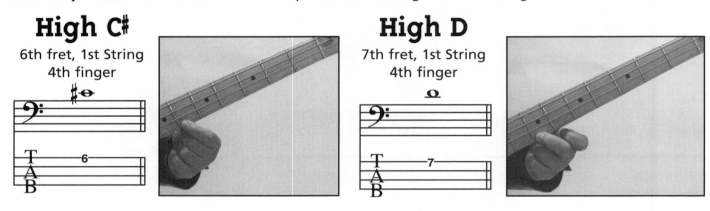

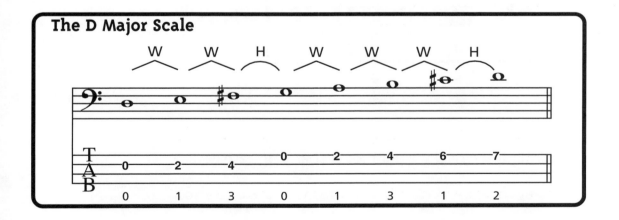

Here is a song that uses the notes of the D Major Scale.

Major Rock

● Triads

A *chord* is three or more notes that are played together. A *triad* is a three-note chord. A major triad is composed of the first, third and fifth notes of a major scale. Below are a few major triads with the major scales they were derived from. Notice that a single letter is used to indicate a major chord above the music. This is called a *chord symbol*. For example, "C" means "C Major chord." Also notice that the scale notes used to create the triads are circled. The lowest note in a triad, the note that gives a chord its name, is called the *root*.

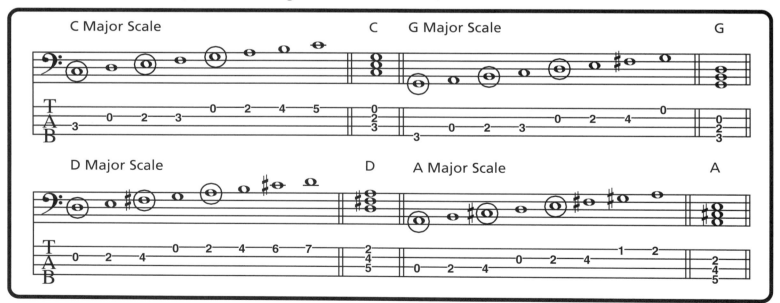

There are hundreds of other chords and types of chords you will need to learn eventually, but for many simple songs, you only need to know a few.

This next song has the chord symbols written above the music. If you are playing with a guitarist, these are suggestions for what he or she might play as you play the bass part. Notice the bass part often uses notes from the indicated chord, and it is most common to play the root. This is not a strict rule, but a starting point for you to create you own bass lines. This is a fast tune.

Track 28

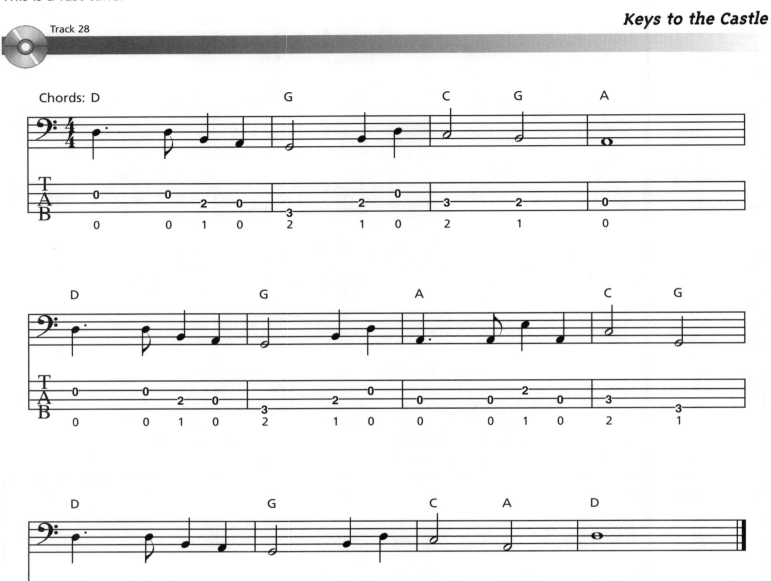

Blues, and Playing with a Guitarist

● Playing the Twelve-Bar Blues

Blues is a simple (although not always *easy*) form of music that is the predecessor to rock, jazz and other forms of popular music. Jam sessions often gravitate toward the blues, because it is something everybody knows.

First, you will need to review three Roman numerals:

Roman Numeral Review
I = 1
IV = 4
V = 5

Important Note:
Each note in a scale is called a *degree*.

In blues, we usually only need three chords for any tune: a chord built on the first degree (I), a chord built on the fourth degree (IV) and a chord built on the fifth degree (V). Here they are in the key of C. A *key* uses the notes of a particular scale, and takes its name from that scale. For example, we say that a piece that uses the notes of the C Major scale is in the key of C Major.

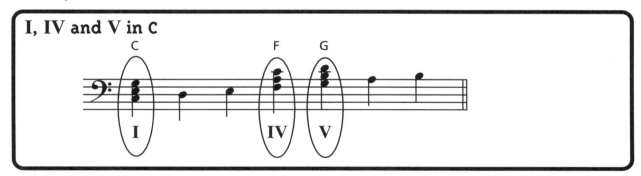

I, IV and V in C

Blues most often takes the form of a *twelve-bar blues* (*bar* is another word for "measure"). This form is so much a part of the blues style that a song arranged this way is often simply called "a blues." You'll often hear musicians say things like, "Hey, let's play a blues in C." Here's the form:

> 4 bars of the I chord
> 2 bars of the IV chord
> 2 bars of the I chord
> 1 bar of the V chord
> 1 bar of the IV chord
> 2 bar of the I chord

Here's a diagram of the twelve-bar blues:

I 1	I 2	I 3	I 4
IV 5	IV 6	I 7	I 8
V 9	IV 10	I 11	I 12

The chords in a G blues would be:

G 1	G 2	G 3	G 4
C 5	C 6	G 7	G 8
D 9	C 10	G 11	G 12

Here is a twelve-bar blues with a *walking bass* part. A walking bass line is a continuous quarter-note part that is common in blues and jazz. Play *Walkin' Talkin' Blues* at a moderate tempo, and try to keep a very steady rhythm. Start walkin'!

Walkin' Talkin' Blues

Track 29

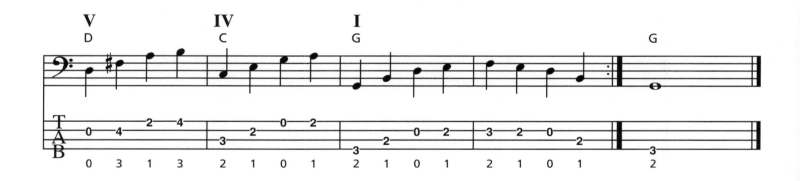

● Other Accidentals—The Flat ♭ and the Natural ♮

The Flat

The flat sign ♭ alters a note by lowering it one fret (one half step). Here are some notes along with their flatted versions. The letters above the staff are the note names.

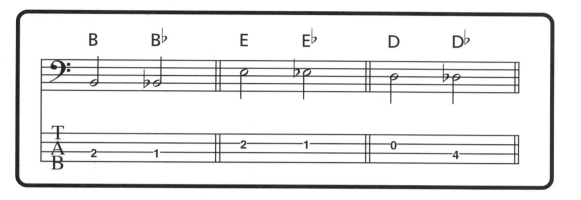

The Natural

The natural sign ♮ cancels the effect of a flat or sharp and returns the note to its original position. Naturals are important since the effect of a sharp or flat continues through to the end of each measure. The only way to cancel the effect of a sharp or flat is to use a natural sign.

For example:

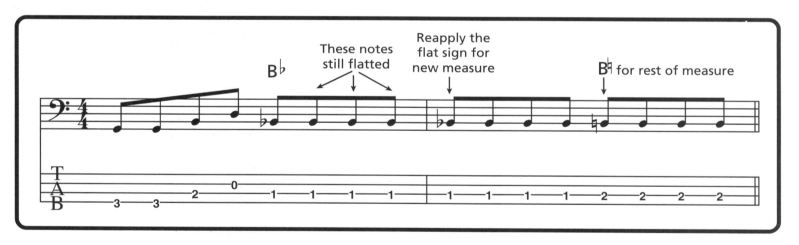

The following is a nice walking bass line with flats and naturals.

Example 9

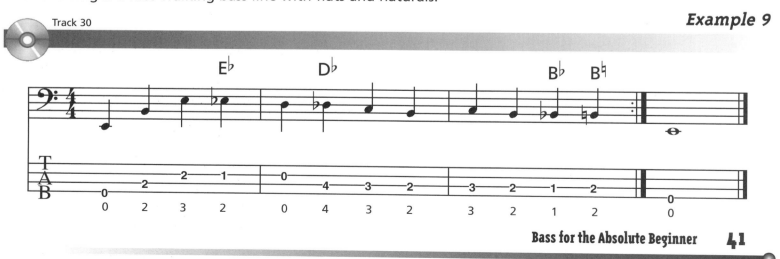

Review Worksheet No. 2

A. Fill in the blank:

1. How many eighth notes can fit into the time of three beats? _____

2. A dot increases the value of a note by _____ its original value.

3. A sharp raises a note and a flat lowers a note by _____ step.

4. In music notation, what do double dots next to a thick/thin double bar line indicate ? _____

5. A whole step is the distance of _____ frets on the bass.

B. Rhythm Review

1. Draw two eighth notes _____ = How many beats?_____

2. Draw a quarter note _____ = How many beats?_____

3. Draw a dotted half note _____ = How many beats?_____

4. Draw a dotted quarter note _____ = How many beats?_____

5. Draw a whole rest _____ = How many beats?_____

C. Scale Review

1. What are the letter names of the notes in a C Major scale?

____ ____ ____ ____ ____ ____ ____ ____

2. What are the letter names of the notes in a G Major scale? (Don't forget the sharp.)

____ ____ ____ ____ ____ ____ ____ ____

3. What are the letter names of the notes in a D Major scale? (Don't forget the sharps.)

____ ____ ____ ____ ____ ____ ____ ____

● Playing with a Guitarist

Since most bass players play with guitarists much of the time, it is a good idea to understand how the guitar works.

The four strings of the bass correspond to the lowest four strings of the guitar. It's just that the bass is tuned one *octave* (twelve half steps) lower. This makes it very easy for a guitarist to show the bassist his notes and vice versa.

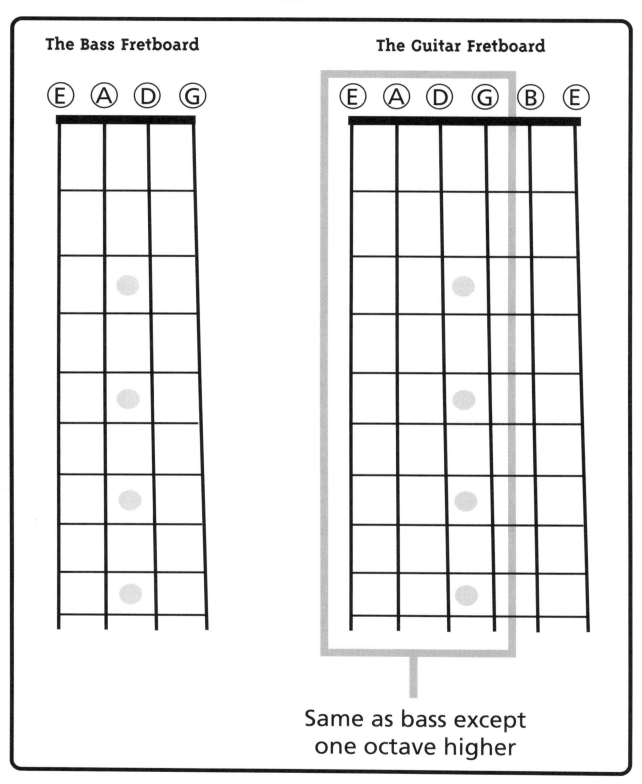

Same as bass except
one octave higher

In rock music , the bass will often double the low strings of the guitar, sounding one octave lower. This makes for very powerful sounding music. Heavy metal groups do this almost all the time.

This song has a bass part that can be easily doubled by the lower strings on the guitar. Play moderately fast and with spirit!

Track 31

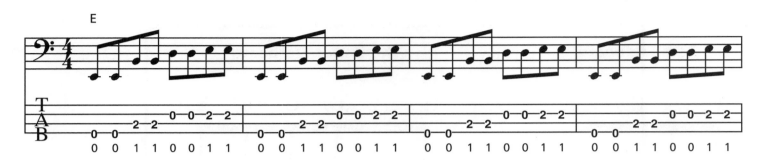

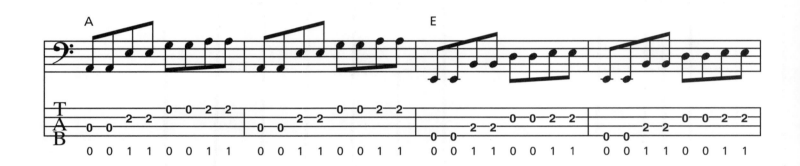

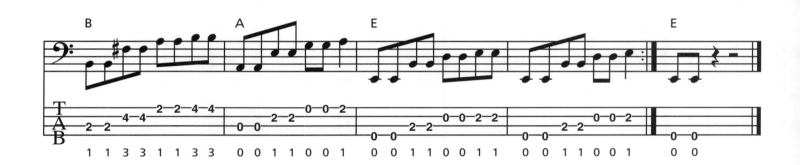

Appendix I—All the Notes on the Bass

Here are all the notes on the bass through the 12th fret, with the accidentals expressed in sharps. Each sharped note has a flat equivalent. For example: A♯= B♭, C♯= D♭, D♯= E♭, F♯= G♭, G♯= A♭ and so on. When two notes have different names but fall on the same fret (have the same pitch), they are said to be *enharmonically* related.

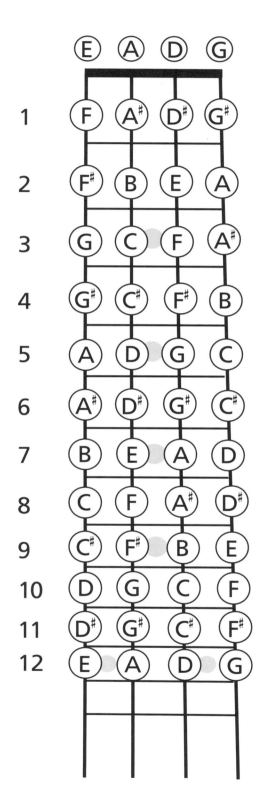

Appendix II–Playing in a Band

Every great band has a bass player who keeps the rhythm solid and shapes the feel of the group. The bass player is the "glue" that holds it all together. No machine can duplicate that human element—the underlying emotional groove—that makes a song magical.

The thrill of playing for an audience is great, whether it is playing to a sold-out house at Madison Square Garden or just a backyard party on a weekend. When people respond, you know you've done your part well. Dig into your instrument and you'll have a great time.

Here are some standard rock songs with solid bass grooves that you should know:

Song	Band
Godzilla	Blue Öyster Cult
Green Onions	Booker T. & the MGs
Louie Louie	The Kingsmen
Money	Pink Floyd
Paranoid	Black Sabbath
Satisfaction	The Rolling Stones
Smells Like Teen Spirit	Nirvana
Whole Lotta Love	Led Zeppelin

Recommended groups for great bass parts:

The Red Hot Chili Peppers
The Rolling Stones
The Beatles
Les Claypool
Primus
Any Motown artist

Now dig in and play!

Answers to Worksheets

Page 20

A. Draw the notes and rests below and tell how many beats.

1. Draw a whole note ○ = <u>4</u> beat(s)

2. Draw a half note = <u>2</u> beat(s)

3. Draw a quarter note = <u>1</u> beat(s)

4. Draw a quarter rest = <u>1</u> beat(s)

5. Draw a half rest = <u>2</u> beat(s)

6. Draw a whole rest = <u>4</u> beat(s)

B. On the TAB below, write the fret number and ther note name of the string it is on.

1. <u>3rd fret, A string</u> 2. <u>2nd fret, D string</u> 3. <u>2nd fret, G string</u> 4. <u>1st fret, E string</u>

C. Fill in the blanks.

1. How many beats are in a measure of 4/4? <u>4</u>

2. In 4/4, what kind of note gets one beat? <u>quarter note</u>

3. What kind of rest gets one beat? <u>quarter rest</u>

4. What kind of rest gets four beats? <u>whole rest</u>

5. When using relative tuning, what fret is used to compare a string with the next string? <u>5th fret</u>

D. Spell words below the staff by writing the note names.

1. <u>D</u> <u>A</u> <u>D</u> 2. <u>E</u> <u>G</u> <u>G</u> 3. <u>F</u> <u>E</u> <u>E</u> <u>D</u> 4. <u>A</u> <u>G</u> <u>E</u>

5. <u>B</u> <u>E</u> <u>G</u> 6. <u>F</u> <u>A</u> <u>D</u> <u>E</u> 7. <u>G</u> <u>A</u> <u>B</u> 8. <u>C</u> <u>A</u> <u>D</u>

Page 42

A. Fill in the blanks.

1. How many eighth notes can fit into the time of three beats? <u>6</u>

2. A dot increases the value of a note by <u>half</u> its original value.

3. A sharp raises a note and a flat lowers a note by <u>one half</u> step.

4. In music notation, what do double dots next to a thick/thin double bar line indicate? <u>repeats</u>

5. A whole step is the distance of <u>2</u> frets on the bass.

B. Rhythm Review

1. Draw two eighth notes. = How many beats? <u>1</u>

2. Draw a quarter note. = How many beats? <u>1</u>

3. Draw a dotted half note. = How many beats? <u>3</u>

4. Draw a dotted quarter note. = How many beats? <u>1½</u>

5. Draw a whole rest. = How many beats? <u>4</u> (or any whole measure)

C. Scale Review

1. What are the letter names of the notes in a C Major scale?

   C D E F G A B C

2. What are the letter names of the notes in a G Major scale? (Don't forget the sharp!)

   G A B C D E F♯ G

3. What are the letter names of the notes in a D Major scale? (Don't forget the sharps!)

   D E F♯ G A B C♯ D